I0211114

# MORNING COMES ROARING DOWN THE MOUNTAIN

*poems by*

## Emily Robyn Clark

*Finishing Line Press*
Georgetown, Kentucky

# MORNING COMES ROARING DOWN THE MOUNTAIN

*For my late father, Albert John Clark*

*"The sweetest thing in all my life has been the longing—
to reach the Mountain, to find the place
where all the beauty came from."*
—C. S. Lewis

## ACKNOWLEDGMENTS

Grateful acknowledgment is made to the editors of the following journals
where the poems in this collection first appeared, sometimes in slightly
altered form:

*Cultural Weekly*: "Luna Moth" and "My Neighbor, Samuel"
*Lavender Review*: "My Muse, My Sun"
*Lullwater Review*: "Maggie the Cat Fights Silence"
*Re-remembering SLCC Community Anthology*: "Body of Water," "Grief:
A Survivor's Tale," "Last Bloom," "Ode to Utah, Land of the Father," and
"Womb of Sorrow"
*The Power of the Feminine "I" Anthology*: "Spiral Goddess" and "My Oracle"
*Spectrum*: "Cascade Springs"

Publisher: Leah Huete de Maines
Editor: Christen Kincaid
Cover Art: Elizabeth Walsh
Author Photo: Erick Wilson
Cover Design: Emily Robyn Clark

Order online: www.finishinglinepress.com
also available on amazon.com

Author inquiries and mail orders:
Finishing Line Press
PO Box 1626
Georgetown, Kentucky 40324
USA

# Contents

## Cascade Springs

Let the wide wild world draw you in like a stone.
Let the bold blue mountain be your comfort, your home.
Let the plums you eat be fresh,
like watercress walking on water
speaking to the air like Juniper flowers.
Take a walk with me there, winding path flower.

## Blue Velvet

I love you for all the reasons
I love this world

brightness in the morning
the dewy earth
limbs down
the big strong
whipping tree wind

the icy feel of rain in May
the blue velvet sky at 9 pm
the way you hold my body in the light.

## East Along the Wasatch

Everything moves east along the Wasatch—
dust, grass, pollen, and the homeless
raised up like the dead
take flight without a word
anything not bolted down
gets carried away.

Light breaks over the peaks
everything left out in the sun fades.

You feel it in your palms
as you head back down the mountain
into fading, deepening blue.

**Pages**

There are pages of
bloody white images in my head
that no one wants to listen to

gunfire, screams, sirens
sex and
torturous nights
of no sleep.

There's a suicide that's not mine
but I can't not see it.

There's death in a move and
a taking of my own life
that hasn't happened yet—

now I'm looking at painted glass
the broken kind
the kind I made into a film
with the actor who wore black so brilliantly
and I'm left holding the pages you ripped from my hands.

## Rings of Grief

Where do I begin?
The page knows my shaking pen

they are circular
these rings of grief tangled in your hair.

I'm spinning now,
walking round and round

beginning at the abuse
then the death of the father

the birth of your love
the eclipsed moon
you asleep in a drug-induced stupor
my father's headstone ordered,
you away in a hospital bed.

Your mail piles up on the counter
night comes swiftly
lightning strikes the mountain.

I read the cards for empathy
your ring never leaves my finger
I devote myself to its symmetry.

The hunter's moon rises
like your father's wrath.

A circle is unbroken and strong because of its shape.
I keep by our bed the letters you made.
There is no end.

## Ode to Utah, Land of the Father

To the woolly land
prickly trees
thorny tall
tempest trees
wide spaces and devouring wind.

I never knew I'd meet you, Utah
you weren't part of my plan
and yet you were the dying light I needed
as the storms raged inside
the rock face I pummeled with my woman's second sight.

You were my dad dying on the table
my lover dying in the doorway

the earthquake shaking me into morning
the cascade of snow I drowned in
halfway skidding off the earth and into a canyon
crying alone in the cold, forbidden aspens.

Wearing a thin leather smile
entering the supermarket on Sundays,
greeted like a ghost.

I was never really here, Utah
I was somewhere else
in a dreamy daze of sun
speckled memories
the eternal beach in my mind.

Yet the languid orange dream
turned to acid
when police haunted our step
and your father cowered below in his car.

I never knew I'd miss you, Utah
and the blue body I saw in the hospital room
the siren of silence under a rising moon
and the pale fever of love descending.

## Last Bloom

I went to visit your rose bushes after you'd gone—
a few were in their last bloom

The yard felt peaceful, everything as it should be:
the sun in its proper place

the tall narrow pine
wind pulling at the aspen

chocolate peppermint along the fence
raspberry bushes overgrown with weeds.

I found your acai berry plant was growing too
and picked a few to taste.

You were remarkable that way
with finding things that didn't fit in;

making the whole mess work in your wild space.

## Morning Comes Roaring Down the Mountain

When we met at a sushi place downtown,
you only told me you left the church.

You didn't tell me about your mother
quietly submitting in the back of the car
Sunday swelling for three hours in the dark icy night,

your only suit jacket
blue patterned and picked out by a stylist because
you didn't want your mother to dress you
as the pills quietly subdued your mind

or how you grew up breathing fumes
from the chemical plant
swirling above the golden angel on the church spire

or how you let the bitterness slip over your tongue
from mushrooms you took while I was in Arkansas.

You do tell me how Jesus stood in front of you
whispering that he is you
as deep gashes appeared on your hands.

Out of the stained glass of your mind's eye
you watched the bent souls of your grandparents
laboring heavy through the wilderness.
You saw yourself as a falling star
in a vast Utah sky.

You didn't tell me that your heart is mostly frozen
only sprouting in places where you want to sing.

One day, waking from your strange sleep
when morning comes roaring down the mountain
tiger-eye gold and gleaming
and the snow falls in April,
you'll remember me.

## Body of Water

My body won't hold any more:
submerged in brackish saltwater,

I'm moved along the slippery ground
pulled roughly like a shell
into an estuary's wide arm.

Here there's only syncopated breath
now with her watery rise and fall
I can't swallow any more.

Swollen eyelids puffy white like milk froth
pilfering seagulls
plunder brown seaweed tangled around my floating belly.

A nick of blood
the salt pierces the wound and I scream
I never knew I could float so long before drowning.

## Confessions

For those of us who never liked me

the frayed moon on Saturday
the shame walk home
alligator boots in the morning

slamming the door on his foot by accident
feeling his anger—
hole punch in the wall.

The dreamy glow of my thighs after sex
the iridescent sheen on my drink

falling asleep at the wheel on the way home
wondering if I'll make it
or if I should swerve off into this car
or stop paying attention for a second and collide.

Wishing I hadn't said that thing
because he no longer texts.

What was it? Did I say something wrong?

The thing wraps around my head
like a snake it circles my throat
and tightens
clenching my airpipe

and I picture how the silk robe
looked on the model
before he hated me in it.

## The Eye

Pulling at the tides,
breaking the backs of the waves
more than once
she exposed me to drowning

but I kept swimming parallel along the shoreline
waiting for her wet eye to stop following

and I made it to the end
the barren cracked soil
I stood up
and walked
the entire way back home alone.

## Luna Moth

The way words fall to the floor
and I hallucinate you in my arms

catching you was so strange
I dreamed you were smaller
curvier than water
and my hands,
ripples down your spine.

I peek into your eyes
and hush
to kiss the eyelids
hovering like a whirring luna moth
over your body

and the wings I disturbed
rested deadly in my arms

you were suffocated under water
and I carried you

wet breasts pushed against my t-shirt
hugging silence

and you lay still on my bed
lips stirring
I murmured back

and hours of sleep draped over us
I spooned you as if you were mine.

## My Neighbor, Samuel

deadbolts the door,
stumbles down three steps.

He'll trip up and down them twenty,
thirty times in the course of an hour.

Samuel's green Converse shoes
thud on the concrete steps.

Watching from my window,
all I can do is stall his compulsion
for a few still minutes
by stepping outside to say hello.

My neighbor says she hears him
sobbing, after he's used up all our water
seeking to sterilize and scourge his skin.

Face down on linoleum,
his suffering seems softer.

# Death Is a Shot in the Dark

*"Ignorance of mortality is a comfort. A man don't have that comfort. He's the only living thing that conceives of death, that knows what it is. The others go without knowing…and yet a pig squeals, but a man sometimes he can keep a tight mouth about it."*
From Tennessee Williams' Cat on a Hot Tin Roof

I schemed my whole life long
born with the strength of seventeen oxen.

I was a mule for hauling bricks, resourceful, iron-clad will.

I worshiped the Earth, she yielded to my pickaxe.
I extracted nectar from her soil—my crops grew lush and full.

Big Mama's lust for finery, sticky on fat fingers
French tapestries, handwoven Persian rugs, silver candlesticks,
porcelain cherubs packed in giant worm-eaten crates
decomposing in my cellar!

I fear the house never belonged to me.
It hurts less, giving it away.

Sometimes I think the world will eat us alive.
I've taken in parts of the globe you never imagined
in your strangest dreams.

Leery, in the streets of Marrakech, I watched a prostitute
under ominous doors
giant doors painted sapphire blue.

Beneath the smoke of my cigar,
a child appeared,
a naked girl with brown eyes
moving toward me.
I fear I've been ripped apart by devils.

As the sun sets over Corsica
I stand on the hotel balcony in my suit
watching light die slowly—
a vibrant sunset sinks into nothingness.

My bare heart envies the vast splaying of color:
opalescent ivory, violet, orange, and pink light
illuminating a revolving cloud bank.

I see the child's disappearing face hidden beneath shadows
and hear the bestial wailings of her mother.
On my plantation, I'm reminded of our own gray battles,
the Confederacy that swallowed my grandfather's generation.

In disintegrating walls of a great house
that never sat quite right—
a crack was in it from the beginning, running up from the cellar,
through the hallways on up the staircase . . . to the bedrooms.

As vines overgrow the house, tenacious fingers climb
on riddling echoing walls, and I know this house
never belonged to me.

The spirits of old Straw and Ochello breathe here—
duality of death and life dwell in this house.

Grandfather Pollitt grew thickness
around his waist and heart after the war.
Constant fighting takes vigor out of a man and he wastes away,
the lifeblood is drained,
that spark of masculine vitality snuffed out on a short wick.

Suddenly, he finds himself a shriveled mass of bones and skin.

Skin so thin it feels heat and cold before new seasons come,
the onset of summer.
He predicts cool autumn winds before they blow in.

The eyeless face of Death appears—and he feels her . . .

hears her

whistling her way through town over train stations and sawmills,
mining pits, and factories,
fields covered with grazing cattle.

Snake-like she weaves, wily over great waters of the Mississippi
over the heads of giant pines, sycamores and poplar trees.
Our fathers and grandfathers planted those trees.

Death feels a hazy layer drift off the meadows at dawn,
she wisps on past the watery heads of flowers drenched in dew.

Death moves into our kitchens, our dining rooms,
our parlors, our sitting rooms, and libraries.
She flies over chandeliers we hung and pianos
we carried in on our own goddam backs!

Death passes over the Smith & Wesson's, Colts, and Winchesters
locked behind glass.
Rifles, shotguns, and pistols lie still in their cases.
Within lethal barrels, the shiny chambers lie vacant
but for a thin layer of black soot
remnants of gunpowder silkier than soil, collecting dust.

She seeps in through floorboards,
slithers into the sleeping arms
of our wives and missus.

I've heard it said a man's purpose
is to suffer valiantly, die unashamed
knowing intimately the thin barrel of his life,
and like a shot fired in the dark he goes—
a smoky plume on a starless night.

But Death is unquieted,
and her thirst unquenchable.

She is the great subduer of men.

## Maggie the Cat Fights Silence

*"Laws of silence don't work . . . When something is festering in*
*your memory or your imagination, laws of silence don't work, it's*
*just like shutting a door and locking it on a house on fire."*
From Tennessee Williams' Cat on a Hot Tin Roof

Along the fertile Delta Big Daddy drew up the lines of his future.

They say it skips a generation—usefulness, that is.

I wore hand-me-down dresses till I got wed.
I fantasized in silk taffeta
the swoosh my legs made when I walked into a room
Mother of Pearl rested so cooly on my neck.

In the suffering room, my lover sleeps in armored chairs
turns his body away from the moon
that cunning stone.

I've dressed the bed in French silk but it swallows me whole.
When I dream I see it all on fire—
flames spinning up the posts
tongues licking the mahogany frame
spooling out onto that cavernous
empty space between my lover and me.

I knew there were big things in store for me:
I read stories in grammar school,
stories of wealth and affluence
like you've never seen in our modern time.

I have plans of my own to recreate the fertile valley,
sequester myself here in this prime piece of real estate
away from mobs clawing at the bars of their own self-made prisons
trampling on each other to get ahead.
I'm going to let these muddy waters flow!

So I went on down to Lowenstein's without Brick knowing
with the intent of picking out a fine gift for Big Daddy
on his birth anniversary.

Brick hasn't the slightest sense to make a gesture.

So here I am, standing on the freshly polished marble
breathing in the candied air from the perfume counter.
I feel hazy—giddy, even.

My, did I lose all sense and think of moving my boudoir in here!
I'm standing in the aisle, running my fingers along the fabrics,
dresses with birds-eye piqué, batiste, silk taffeta, bouclé sweaters
of mohair and wool.

Lingerie calls my name.
I long to feel ivory lace,
lace over my mouth,
lace brushing over my lips.

I watch husbands and lovers moving in the warm room
choosing corsets and silky things,
anniversary gifts, secret presents, too.

I imagine I'm carried away screaming
pulled by the hair
fucked in the dark!

Brick's hands are numb.
I know, but I haven't felt them.
My husband is Achilles, disappointment to the gods.

I finger a lilac chemise pooling on the table.
The clerk's pale, sunken eyes follow me.

Rain guards the long drive to Big Daddy's house
drenches everything in its fury—
not even a stone remains
and the garden's washed out by morning.

Brick labors on a wet, grassy field:
he's training for immortality he tells me.
His body moves without his mind.

He's a typhoon, a gladiator
with no crowd to condemn him.

At night I lie awake listening to his breath, a slow painful suction.
His helmet, scarlet red—
I swear it speaks to him when I'm not around!

He sits in convulsive silence.
his large hands make the glass sweat.
He stares, a sniper ready to kill.

I slip on a powder pink nightgown with eyelet cutouts
and white bows soft as my own dove hands.
I listen for the tinseled voice of our unborn child

but my womb's a dying ember, a dwarf star burning out
to a single amber glow.

I close the rose silk drapes and wait in the dark.

## Grief: A Survivor's Tale

"May I grieve with you?" said Maus, "my book is banned."
Some cannot resist the desire to shut their eyes to the Horror

Nazi horror,
no mercy in it
spilling incessantly
rivers of black blood
pooling around our feet leaving us gagging, gasping.

There is something to the looking at, acknowledging
but no one wants to see or get their hands dirty.

Somehow we are defiled in the witnessing,
the viewing, the reading of the truth of it.
In our voyeurism,
through broken eyes we see and want to escape
but it's our human weight to bare

singed flesh, melting hours, those heavy clocks in the sky
tolling the inhuman hour.

Poe saw it and felt it before his corpse lay in the street.
The writer slandered him
but the horror had its revenge and he was rectified,
deified post-mortem.
Somehow his stories did not cut our flesh the way true ones do

the way your hand collapsed in mine when I held it tight
you far away in a dark dream
me waiting for a nurse to tell
how close you are to the horrible hour.

## My Oracle

*"Long shall I rue thee,
Too deeply to tell."*
                    *"When We Two Parted"* —Lord Byron

My oracle, find me here
Under the tawdry pink tulle of her dress
Speaking mindlessly into the folds,
Spreading her arms like wings on the pillow.
She leads me into Newstead Abbey's Great Hall
Where my portrait tilts on a single nail
And I aim arrows to slice open the ancestral dark
That clings to the crumbling stone.

The gallery mocks me.
A chorus of sirens reaches out with silver hooks to cut me.
The artist has painted me wrong—
what gall to show my obscene Oedipus foot!
My Deity, rise up from your lake of silence
And follow me into exile.
The boat is moored—listen, I can hear wings stirring,
Lifting off the surface.

In the brothel's swamp-light I coin a greater light,
A lock of your hair stowed like gold in my purse.
In the half-lit space I move, slowly toward the wall of women
Waiting for a gesture.

Barmaid, refill my glass of bitters!
I look past the smoldering flame, past women like fixtures
Plastered to the dark.

The star of my cheek
Is not burning for passion tonight, not
This passion. It burns only for you, my love.
Darling, let me dream
The lamb-white ribbon of your dress,
Feel your curls like a silken crescent angled around your face.

My goddess, stand with me on the Grecian shore,
Pluck the brass buttons from my coat, thrust the pen
From my fingers.

Swallowed up in a surge of iron sea,
I walk beside Greek warriors in chariots,
Flaming darts rising from the sea floor.

You are bliss,
My temple forever.

## My Muse, My Sun

Moving onto my lap,
your body blooms

I feel powerless
floating
on a great ocean
under you, the sun

when we lie naked,
my fingers search
for ports of call.

Every exploration begins with a question
and you murmur, "yes"

It's pure revelation,
this skin—

I wear darkness on my sleeve
like rhythmic night,
peyote in the crescent deep,
I steal kisses and hope you swear to me alone:

I'm your holiday forever.

## Behind Her Eyes Are Petals

A girl
barely yellow
is cushioned in a corner

she drinks champagne from crystal
smoke undulates on blond strands
a black clove cigarette rests between two fingers
the ceiling fan whirs incessantly.

Startled in her glass frame
I first notice—
bold blue slippers on delicate feet
some words give way,
and she opens the door.

I search with my hands on her back,
she tells me not to stop.
A cold pocket of rain regards us
my singing hands stroke on
and fingers pulse electric on her scalp
concentric thoughts give way to her
even stones wear down to pebbles in this current.

It's thunderous outside
a zig zag catches my eye
jagged, narrow veins emerge on maps of sky.

She disappears in blankets
I'm staring at her walls now
no one questions why she dresses in army gray and navy blue.
When she's sleeping, my mind is on her whirring ceiling.

Fall cools everything
I see her stripped of all but smoke
she's still inhaling
behind her eyes are petals:
Monet painted her this way.

## For the Memory of Her
*For Savannah*

Of all the colors
yours is the most real

I'm staring through fractals
waiting for you to appear

deciphering the human body
the gestures
a crooked smile
parted lip
a spark of the eye.

Only with you
does this flavor of blue
rise like steam off the bath.

I think of all the places
I haven't shown you

faces I could've revealed
if you'd let me
see more of you

learn to read your mind's eye
a sparrow perched
between branches
surveying where to climb

I'm starting to forget now
the little parts of you—
the mole on your shoulder, or was it your arm?
you're fading a little every day.

When I go out into the world,
stopping to look through a glass shop window
I'm starting to see my own face again.

When I look at the photos,
I remember that you were with me
and that you didn't like to,
but you smiled for me.

## Womb of Sorrow

I'm bringing my body back into the world
from where it was so small
malformed in the womb of sorrow.

Traffic lights in the city downtown
stream over my face like kind water
and I see the road ahead again.

Pain is a kind of slowing cello
low and trembling in the ear
like the earth below
other taller, brighter things.

Pain is a kind of shadow body—
its pallid fingers strangle the soul.

Strange, stillborn, it doesn't heed gravity
and waits to silence the firstborn.

The two, cheek by jowl in the belly
until one swallows the other.

## Spiral Goddess

*"The eternal feminine draws us on."*
*—Johann Wolfgang von Goethe*

### I

The goddess knows when the rain comes.
She plants seeds in deep mystery
where dreams weave and animals speak:
her womb is infinity.

We drum and hold seance in the dark
thunder rolls and we bow to the earth bent like ancient trees.
The rain appears
thick and delicious on our skin
our arms like wheat shoot to the cerulean sea,
swirling in spirals above.

When the goddess is silent
we study constellations to see her vision,
painted light stretched across eternity.

### II

Columbia is tethered to our altar
She wants to cry out her name:
"Justice, the Guardian of Liberty"!
but her mouth is frozen shut on the cold marble slab.
Women's intuition said this would happen:
A virgin goddess chosen as the figurehead of our nation—
Columbia born between Virginia and Maryland
so eerily familiar to one Virgin Mary.

Now the law books read:
impure, unchaste, unclean
are the bearing, fertile, pregnant citizens.

The goddess is starved, hung out naked,
bled out in a nightmare scene—a handmaid's tale.

But listen, Lysistrata may awaken soon
breed the growing thirst for Her blood
by kindling a hunger strike, a righteous fast.
Famished, men will die,
bleached bones under white sheets.

It is the goddess who begins the spiral, circle of a nation's life.

### III

The hero's journey begins at Her feet:
the great goddess Hera took pity on Zeus as a bird and wed him,
and Inanna sacrificed her own life for her lover, Tammuz.
Descending to the underworld,
she traded all worldly goods for him.

The goddess is all consuming,
her love, oceanic.
She is the burning sun
bearer and begetter of all things,
destroyer of worlds.

Her name is Isis, Ishtar, Inanna, Astarte
she offers fruit from the Tree Eternal
she is the bounds of space and time.

She is wild, feline,
a cosmic serpent
she is the ground you stand on
the spiral that swings the world.

## The Dream

I am a whirl in a cycle
a star circling a storm

I am the blue morning
the abyss
a dream within a well

the rise of the moon over a palm,
light fading out and levitating over the trees.

## With Thanks

I'm thankful for all those who have contributed to my growth and success as a poet.

Special thanks to the fellowship and community I found with Ventura County poets, including former Ventura County Poet Laureate Mary Kay Rummel, Richard Newsham, Phil Taggart, Marsha de la O, Brad Bauer, Friday Gretchen, and Ventura Arts Council for their support. Thanks to my Los Angeles friends and mentors Laurie O'Brien and Carl Weintraub for helping to revive my love of performance poetry, and to my friends Jessica Wilson and Juan Cardenas at Los Angeles Poet Society for their friendship and support. I'm grateful for the incredible organization California Poets in the Schools and the poet teachers who inspired me to teach, including my poetry mentor, the late John Oliver Simon, and poet friends Jim Cartwright, Sue Terence, Ariel Fintushel, and the late Shelley Savren. I'm grateful for Lisa Max Zimet and The Aspen Poets' Society for their friendship and for publishing my work, and to my poet friend William Cushing for reading and championing my words, and to musician and trailblazer Nathan McEuen, who encouraged my poetry writing and publishing and offered me the stage to perform with him many times in venues across the U.S. Also, I wish to thank Fish Burton for his depth of insight and intuition in reading my poetry and my mother, Arkansas Poet Laureate Suzanne Rhodes, for her encouragement, eye for detail, and championing of my poetry.

I'm grateful to Leah Huete de Maines, publisher of Finishing Line Press, for believing in my work.

**Emily Robyn Clark** is an award-winning poet, poetry teacher, and author of the poetry collection *Art Triumphant* (2017).

Clark's poetry has been featured in *Lullwater Review, Askew, A! Magazine, Spectrum, The Sow's Ear Poetry Review, The Power of The Feminine "I," Re-Remembering, a Community Anthology, Lavender Review, Aspen Daily News, LA's Cultural Daily*, and *Ventura Emerging Poet Series*.

She has performed her poetry all over the United States, making appearances at such notable venues as SoHo in Santa Barbara, Beyond Baroque in Venice, The Victory Theatre Center in Burbank, the Ojai Art Center in Ojai, Weller Book Works in Salt Lake City, and The Aspen Poets' Society in Aspen.

Clark taught poetry workshops for four years in Ventura, California, to middle and high school students through California Poets in the Schools, one of the oldest writer-in-residency programs in the country. Commissioned by the Ventura Arts Council, she published a student anthology called *Tasty Little Samples*, featuring the work of 70 students she taught through workshops at Balboa Middle School and Buena High School.

In addition to her work as a poet, she is also an award-winning filmmaker, fiction writer, journalist, and singer-songwriter who goes by the stage name Emma Dream.

A native of Bristol, Tennessee, known as the birthplace of country music, Clark has since lived and worked in Virginia, Oregon, Utah, California, Florida, and Europe throughout her adult life but believes Southern California feels most like home. She currently lives in Florida where she studied in the MFA program in Film Production at Florida State University's College of Motion Picture Arts.

Clark is a feminist who is deeply passionate about human rights, social justice, and advocating for marginalized communities. In her personal life, she enjoys painting, studying philosophy, and researching ancient history and esoteric traditions. A practicing Buddhist and light worker, she embraces a healing path while remaining dedicated to uplifting society's underdogs.

www.ingramcontent.com/pod-product-compliance
Lightning Source LLC
Chambersburg PA
CBHW022044080426
42734CB00009B/1227